Buying the Perfect RV

Raymond Laubert

Published by Laubert Enterprises, 2015.

While every precaution has been taken in the preparation of this book, the publisher assumes no responsibility for errors or omissions, or for damages resulting from the use of the information contained herein.

BUYING THE PERFECT RV

First edition. June 18, 2015. Copyright © 2015 Laubert Enterprises

Written by Raymond Laubert

About the Author

Raymond Laubert is a Certified Recreational Vehicle Inspector. He is trained and certified by the National Recreational Vehicle Inspectors Association (NRVIA). He has written many articles for the novice on Facebook and on the RV Inspecting Service website. Ray is retired Air Force, were he performed as an electronics trainer for several years. He a veteran of the Gulf War. During his 21 years of service, he was stationed in Japan, Saudi Arabia as well as several state side bases. Upon retirement, he became a Microsoft Certified System Engineer, Microsoft Certified Database Administrator and Microsoft Certified Trainer. He has written many articles for public use and has published two books up until now. The "Is It the Perfect RV" series is scheduled to be 4 books that will take the novice recreational or camping reader from finding the perfect RV, through inspection, packing, using and maintaining the recreational vehicle. Ray has been married to Daisy since 1972 and together they have 4 children, 10 grand children and 2 great grand children. They are currently traveling around the country in their RV with two small dogs, Princess and Misty. You can follow their adventures at http://our-rv-adventures.com.

Table of Contents

Introduction 6

Overview 6

Equipment 8

Timing 9

Roof Inspection 11

Exterior Sidewalls 13

Chassis Inspection 18

    Tires 20

    Levelers, Jacks and Stabilizers 24

    Engine and Transmission 25

Electrical Systems 26

    Generator 29

    Inverter 31

    Converter 31

Water Systems 32

    Water Heater 33

    Waste Water System 35

Propane /LP/ CO / Smoke Detectors 35

    LP Detector 37

    Smoke Detector 37

    CO Detector 38

Appliances 39

    Refrigerator 39

    Furnace 40

    Cook Top 40

    Air Conditioner 41

Interior 41

    Ceiling, Walls and Floor 41

    Cabinets 42

    Blinds and Shades 42

    Furniture 43

Checklist 45

Introduction

Buying the Perfect RV is mainly about making sure you are getting a good sound and operational recreational vehicle. We are going to be inspecting all major components of the RV inside and out. By the time this is over, you will have a good understanding of the unit and it's operation.

Overview

To do the inspection right you will need several hours for two people. The inspection requires no special tools and some areas will not be inspected as thoroughly as a professional RV Inspector would do. RV Inspectors are trained to use special equipment to check propane, electric, heating and cooling systems. Since some people using this guide will not have that training, I have left those areas to the professionals.

If you are interested in having a professional inspection performed please visit our website at http://rv-inspection-service.com and click on the link for RV Inspections or send an email to

During the inspection you will be looking at all major subsections of the RV from the roof to the frame and most parts in between. Having a camera with you is a good idea. Take pictures of anything that doesn't look right or is clearly broken. You can review these later with a professional to determine if anything needs to be addressed. In addition, it is a good idea to photograph any make, model and serial numbers you find. These can be used to help order new parts and for insurance purposes.

The inspection process is not rocket science. Basically, it is up to you to determine if something is acceptable or not. As a Certified RV inspector, I will look at something differently than you might. You may have a strong background in carpentry, for example, and decide that any wood work you would be willing to do and decide that a weak trim board is acceptable, whereas I would note it as Needs Repair. I tried to design the rating system as simple as possible. Yes/No or Acceptable/Needs Repair are the most common ratings. If you feel because of the age and deal you are getting that something is 'to be expected' and are willing to live with it or fix it yourself, rate it as Acceptable and move on. However, if you think something needs to be repaired mark it as such and discuss this with the seller. Maybe for a few dollars discount you will both agree that you can take care of it. In the end this is a guide to help you look at all the major areas of the recreational vehicle before you spend any money. This inspection is a PRE Sale inspection not something you do once you have laid down your hard earned money.

Equipment

You will need a few tools to do the inspection.

A Ladder to climb onto the roof or to inspect the slide outs and roof. Yes most recreational vehicles have ladders but these are not the safest things in the world. If you weigh less than 150 lbs. you can probably use the ones attached to the recreational vehicle but if you weigh more than that or if the ladder appears to be less than safe, you will want something different to access the roof area. The roof IS the most important part of the inspection. Most major issues start with a problem on the roof.

A set of screwdrivers both Phillips and Flathead. Some access panels will require you to remove some screws. No major disassembly of the recreational vehicle will be required.

A flashlight. Some areas of the recreational vehicle like under the sink and behind the refrigerator will be pretty dark. So a good flashlight with fresh batteries will help a lot.

A camera. Your cell phone or an inexpensive digital camera will do. Anything that can be used to take a picture for reference. You will want a picture of anything that doesn't look right.

Tablet, clipboard and pencil. You will need these to take notes and to fill out the check list.

Oil/Fluid Sample Kits and draw pump. If you are purchasing a motorized recreational vehicle, you will need some sample kits. These can be gotten from http://www.jglubricantservices.com/online_store.html. Oil and Coolant kits will run about $56.00 plus shipping. If the unit has a generator you will want to perform the analysis on it as well. The analysis takes a couple of days plus shipping time. So it is best to make the sale contingent on the results. A down payment should solve any issue with the seller. If they are not willing to wait, you probably don't want that unit.

One playing card. This will be used to check seals around the slide outs.

Three prong electrical tester. This will be used to check the polarity and operation of the AC circuits.

Optional, Thermometer. A digital thermometer will allow you to check the temperatures of the refrigerator, hot water, microwave operation and air conditioners.

Timing

To perform this inspection I would plan on at least 4 to 6 hours to perform the inspection. You will want electrical power, water, and sewer hooked up. If possible have the refrigerator turned on at least 4 hours ahead of time. You want at least 1/4 tank of fuel to test the generator operation if one is installed. The recreational vehicle should be set up, level and jacks/stabilizers/levelers down. If any of these cannot be done, some of the inspection items will not be able to be completed.

A recreational vehicle inspection report is the result of a visual inspection of the structure and components of an RV at a specific point in time. You will be looking at the RV to see that all systems are performing correctly and safely. If a problem or a symptom of a problem is found, you will note the issue in the guide and include a description of the problem. The owner does not need to be present during the inspection but it is often helpful if the seller or a representative attends the inspection. Performing this inspection yourself is an excellent way to learn about the recreational vehicle even if no problems are found.

The inspection will cover the following systems in the recreational vehicle.

Roof – materials, penetrations, attachments, antennas, vents, air conditioners, general condition.

Exterior – surfaces, doors, windows, steps, tires, jacks, levelers, awnings, slide toppers, decals, paint.

Electrical – AC/DC, Converters, Inverters, fuse and circuit breaker panels, ground fault receptacles, wiring, switches, lighting fixtures, outlets, smoke detectors.

Heating and Cooling – operating controls, furnaces, boilers, fans, ducts, filters, shutoff switches and valves.

Plumbing – shut off valves, water supply piping, drain and waste piping, valves, faucets, leaks, toilets.

Interior – floors, walls, ceiling and trim, counters, cabinets, door and window operation.

Propane - detectors, stove, heater, water heater, gas pressure, tanks and much more.

A recreational vehicle inspection is not protection against future failures, nor does it provide a warranty against future problems The inspection reveals the condition of the component at the time the component was inspected. For protection from future failure you may want to consider a RV Extended Warranty.

Roof Inspection

When looking into buying an RV start with a roof inspection. The vast majority of problems with any recreational vehicle start with problems on the roof, yet the majority of buyers never even see the roof. They are interested in what is inside the recreational vehicle.

Damage to a roof leads to water getting into the walls and flooring, causing things to slowly rot away from the inside out. It may take years before the damage is seen and by then it will be too late to repair it. A simple branch scraping across the roof can rip a small hole into the fabric that covers the recreational vehicle. Water will find it's way into the roof and begin it's journey to the floor.

You will need to bring a ladder. Trust me, the ones that are attached will not be good enough unless you weigh less than 150 lbs. Once you are on the roof stay on your hands and knees. Why? For two reasons. One is safety. It is hard to fall when you are already down. Plus you are on 4 points of contact, so even if you should get too close to the ledge, you have a better chance to recover than if you are upright. The second reason to be on your hands and knees is to put you closer to the stuff you are inspecting. It is much easier to see things up close than from 5 ft. away while standing.

Once you are on the roof, start in one corner on your hands and knees and inspect all of the roof. Looking for holes, torn material, caulking that is peeling apart, broken vents or AC covers, etc. If the unit has slides, check the seals while they are in and out. If you find something that doesn't look right, make a note, take a picture and check the inside very carefully in that area when you get down.

While you are on the roof, check for anything that might indicate repairs have been performed. Look for the different antennas (Radio, Satellite, TV, etc). Pay attention to any seals. Remember if in doubt record and photograph it. Look at all the covers on the roof. You will have vents, fans, air conditioning covers, at a minimum. You may also have refrigerator vents in some units.

Look at the slide toppers if your unit has them. Are they secure? Are they showing signs of wear? If the slide does not have slide toppers check the rubber seal along the top of the slide. Also look at the top of the slide. Any holes or repairs?

Look for areas on the roof where water seems to collect. These will be easy to spot as a dip or darker spot in the roof material. Finally, as you crawl around on the roof, check for soft spots. Note these and photograph them as well. If at any time you sink into the roof, back away slowly, get down from the roof and thank the seller while telling them you are NOT interested in this recreational vehicle. The roof has probably started to rot away and the cost to repair is not worth your time or money.

Exterior Sidewalls

When you come down from the roof, start in the same corner you started from on the roof. Look down the length of the recreational vehicle and look for bumps or imperfections in the walls. Especially in areas where you might have found water or holes on the roof. This could be a sign of delamination. If you find spots that you are concerned about. Note the location, photograph it and find a third party to inspect it. I have a series of articles on delamination on the website at RV Inspection Service. There are now several manufacturers that offer kits to repair minor delamination issues. However, this is a major problem and probably a deal breaker.

Now slowly walk around the rig and look at the windows, seals, entrance way for signs of damage or repairs. Look at the overall condition of the windows, glass, walls, decals etc. Note any issues and take a picture.

If there are cargo doors on the side you are inspecting, check for their operation. Do they lock and unlock? Check the inside of the door for rust. Note the type of lock. Be aware that most recreational vehicles use the same set of keys. Travel trailers and fifth wheels use the same keys in the storage areas and motorized recreational vehicles will use another. If security is important to you, you will want to change out the locks.

If there are window awnings or door awnings you will want to look at the mounting hardware and material. Are they in good shape? Is the awning material torn? What kind of drive mechanism is there? Is it in good shape? Does it operate on electric, manual or connected to the slide? Do they all work?

Using the ladder you want to inspect all the window seals. This is a common area for leaks and will not be seen from the inside. Water will leak down, around the window frame and into the walls. Usually causing delamination. Again this is a simple fix with any good silicone sealer that is rated for outdoor use.

Entry Steps and Doors are next. You want to make sure that the steps operate properly. If they are electric, there will be a lock out switch somewhere inside the unit. Test to make sure that it operates properly, preventing the stairs from extending. Check for excessive signs of rust. Check to make sure the stairs retract fully.

For the door, make sure that the keys work. Check around the window for any signs of leaking.

Section 4 of the checklist deals with slide outs. However, since you are already walking around the vehicle anyway it is a good time to talk about this area of inspection.

Slide outs create a much need living space in the recreational vehicle. They are, however, holes in the side walls of the vehicle and as such create a unique set of problems. There are seals that are in use when the slide is in and another set of seals in use when the slide is out. Both of these seals are equally important. In addition, there is a mechanical device that pulls the slides in and pushes the slide out. As with all things mechanical it can break or get out of whack. So special care must be given when inspecting the slide outs.

Starting with the box, which is basically all the slide out is. Inspect the walls, roof, sides and undercarriage for any defects, holes, patches etc. Look for repairs that have been made. There will be some kind of mechanism that will pull/push the slide out in and out of the RV. There are currently three major types, electrical, hydraulic and geared. It really doesn't matter to you or for this inspection which type you have. You want to make sure that the slides go in and out EVENLY. With the slide all the way in, stand outside and look at where the seals meet the wall of the slide and the wall of the recreational vehicle. Are there any gaps? I like to use a playing card to see if I can slip it between the two walls. As long as it takes the same pressure to push it in, I am fine. When it slides in easily in one area or with no friction at all then there is an adjustment to be made. Indicate it on the report. If you find that one side is out of whack with the other, note it as well. This is also an adjustment. These are not major issues in most cases, just adjustments that need to be made. You want to make sure that the seals are all compressed. Otherwise water will leak in while you are driving or while in storage and cause damage to the slide or recreational vehicle.

Now extend the slide. It is best to have two people for this. One inside extending the slide and the other outside to watch the movement of the slide. You are looking for a smooth, consistent operation. With the slide all the way out, look at the seals from both inside and outside. Are they compressed? Again with a playing card, I try to slide it between the seal and the wall from the inside. It should not slide in. If it does the slide isn't all the way out or needs adjustment. Our 2007 Safari had a problem with the road side slide. You could actually see outside behind the driver's seat. It was a simple adjustment, but it let all kinds of water seep into the rig as well as bugs.

Check under the slide outs. Here you are looking for damage, both by water and accidents. Check for excessive rust. If the slide has a topper (awning), check the material and connections. Check for rusty or corroded screws and bolts. With a ladder, check the top of all the windows. See if they need caulking and check for water damage.

Check all the appliance doors. These include the hot water heater, refrigerator and heaters. Make sure they all operate as required.

Check all of the awnings. Look for pin-holes in the awning material. Operate the awning(s) to make sure it(they) retract(s) completely. Check that the metal components are in good shape and work normally.

Chassis Inspection

Regardless of the type of rig you are buying the chassis is an important area to inspect. It is exposed to the elements and, like the roof, very few buyers or owners ever take a look at the chassis. Where the roof is the source of most damage to the recreational vehicle the chassis is the foundation of the rig. A poor foundation means that the RV will have a short or shorter life.

First I want to cover items that are common to all recreational vehicles. The frame and the stabilizers/ jacks/levelers. You will need to get down and dirty here. Climb under the rig and look at the frame. Look for signs of rust, damage, bent or broken connections, welds that are broken etc. Look for signs of rubbing or excessive wear. Check around the tires for grease, brake fluid and other lubricants. Anything seem excessively wet or dry? Both of these conditions can indicate problems. Excessively wet could indicate a leak and excessively dry could indicate poor maintenance. As part of this inspection you are not required to take anything apart. But just like your car, the recreational vehicle will require maintenance by a qualified mechanic. This might be a good time to have one inspect the frame, brakes and other mechanical areas.

Look around the tire wells for signs of damage. It is not uncommon for tires to blow out and the treads to cause damage that might be hidden from casual inspection.

Although not actually under the carriage, check all of the lights. These include the brakes, running lights, backup lights, exterior lights and entrance lights. Are all bulbs working? Some of the new lights are LED and made up of multiple sets of LED. If all are lit then good, if the majority are lit, then I would pass it with a note. If less than half are missing then I would require them to be replaced.

If the RV has a trailer hitch, you want to make sure that it is working and has all the parts are there See if there is documentation or a sticker on the capacity of the hitch. You want to make sure that you do not exceed the hitch rating regardless of the capabilities of the unit.

Tires

There is so much that you need to be aware of when purchasing an RV about tires, that I find I am in overload just trying to put it in terms everyone will understand.

Tires are one of the areas that we seem to overlook. Many people, both experienced, and inexperienced fail to pay attention to and suffer the consequences of their oversight.

Tire issues are not a problem only with used units. So let me start with the basics. Many manufacturers are overlooking or worse disregarding the proper tire use on the RVs they are making. So let me start this series of articles with the basics. Please bear with me, I will probably cover things you already know, but I want to make sure we are all on the same page.

Tires for RVs are not the same as tires for your car or truck. These are considered Special Purpose tires. The tires have several things we want to look for. They include the load range, the age, the pressure, the tread and size.

Tire Pressure

You will want to take the tire pressure. A good truck tire pressure gauge will be a worthwhile investment. The pressure of the tire determines how much weight it can carry. Under inflated tires reduce the amount of weight they can handle, which will lead to the tire failing causing a blowout. I have a whole series of tire articles on the website at http://rv-inspection-service.com.

Next thing to look at is the tread. Most RVs do not have a problem with the amount of tread left on the tire. But just in case you get a hold of a well traveled rig, the depth of the tread should be greater than 3/16 th of an inch and evenly worn across the tire.

Load Range

The Department of Transportation requires that all tires have certain information branded into the side walls of the tires. The load range/ply rating identifies how much load the tire is designed for at its maximum pressure. ST or Special Trailer service tires are rated one of these values.

B 4 ply Max Pressure 35 PSI
C 6 ply Max Pressure 50 PSI
D 8 ply Max Pressure 65 PSI
E 10 ply Max Pressure 80 PSI
F 12 ply Max Pressure
G 14 ply Max Pressure
H 16 ply Max Pressure
J 18 ply Max Pressure
L 20 ply Max Pressure
M 22 ply Max Pressure
N 24 ply Max Pressure

Search as I might, I could not find the maximum tire pressure for ratings F-N. Other than 120 PSI being the highest PSI. So please check the tires you have on the RV for maximum PSI.

Age

This is the area that gets most of us. We are used to our cars and running the tires until they are bald. When we look at a used RV the tires seem great! But remember these are Special tires. They are not designed like our car and truck tires. Car and truck tires have UV protection built into the side walls and rubber. This prevents the sun from damaging the tires structure and makes them last longer. ST tires do not have this special protection. As such the sun damages the tires when they are exposed. Depending on who you listen to, the ST tires will last a few as 5 years before needing to be replaced to as many as 10 years. I have found nothing that says always change the tire after x number of years. But the apparent wisdom is no more than 7 years. So how do you determine the age of the tire?

On one side of the tire you will find the DOT information. The last four digits will be the birth date of the tire. The first two digits are the week of the year and the last two digits are the year. So a tire date code of 4312 would be the 43rd week of 2012. Add 7 to that and this tire would need to be changed out by 4319 or the 43rd week of 2019.

Inspection. So now that you know what to look for it is time to inspect those tires. I would recommend that you bring a piece of white chalk to mark the area where the size, load range, date and max pressure will be found. Some of this information will only be printed on one side of the tire. Murphy's Law says it will be the inside of the tire. Get on the ground and carefully search the tire until you find the information.

Record it as best you can. Take the tire pressure as well. Remember, this might be less than maximum but can be adjusted.

Inspect the side walls of all the tires both inside and outside. Look for cracks, tears, gauges etc. If you find any, I would replace the tire.

Now find the weight sticker for the unit. This will be either in the cab area behind or next to the driver's seat or on a tow-able it will be curbside near the front of the unit. Write down the maximum weight the unit is designed to handle. You want the highest value you can find on the chart. Now for some research. Look up the make, model, size, etc. of the tire on the manufacturers website. Compare the maximum rating of the tire with the maximum rating of the RV. IF the RV is heavier, the tires are no good and will need to be replaced. Do not let anyone tell you differently. An overweight rig will cause the tires to fail and that could cost you your life.

Levelers, Jacks and Stabilizers

Check the jacks/levelers for operation. Make sure they perform as required. Manual jacks are not meant to raise or lower the unit, only to stabilize or reduce the movement of the unit when extended. Hydraulic jacks found on motor homes will literally raise the unit off the tires, but this is not recommended for long term use. For safety reasons, do not use levelers to change tires. Prior to operating any hydraulic unit, make sure that the pump has enough oil/fluid.

For levelers you will want to check the fluid levels in the hydraulic chamber. One final check will be with the levelers extended. Check to see if the steel cylinders are clean and rust free. Levelers are not met to be extended for long periods of time. If the rig was used by a full timer in FL for 6 months at a time, the levelers may have rust on them which will eat the seals and require replacing them. The elements are not friendly to steel. Salt from the sea or ice melting compounds are not their friends.

For levelers with air/hydraulic systems, you want to make sure the air pressure system works and that the storage tank is free of moisture. There should be an air purge valve on the tank. You will need to open it at some point in the inspection to test for moisture. If in doubt, have a mechanic look over the system.

Engine and Transmission

Now I know that travel trailers and fifth wheels don't have engines, but all of the 'Class' types of recreational vehicles do. So this section is for them. There is only one test that I feel you can do that will truly tell you what shape the engine and transmission is in, and that is the fluid analysis. In my opinion you must perform these tests. These are easy to do, but will cost you a few dollars. You will need a draw pump and the sample kits. Perhaps a local service station will do the test for you. If the rig is a diesel, spend the money. You will perform the analysis every year and save a lot of money on fluid changes.

Treat the recreational vehicle engine and transmission like you would buying a used car. Check the belts, electrical connections, batteries, antifreeze, oil, maintenance records etc. Look for oil leaks on the engine and on the ground. When was the engine last serviced?

If the oil has been recently changed, do not bother with an oil analysis. Anything less than 1,000 miles will not provide the details that an analysis is good for. If the seller has maintenance records showing consistent maintenance that this is probably not a bad thing. I am leery of an engine that has no maintenance records and fresh oil. In this case, I would make sure to do a transmission and antifreeze analysis at a minimum. Often the antifreeze will provide some indication of pending problems. Let the buyer beware is good advice to go by. Many times you can tell if the previous owner took good care of the vehicle by how clean it is. That is another indication you would want to note on the report.

If any fluids are low or do not show up on the dipstick, make a note and in my opinion would be cause to look for another unit.

Electrical Systems

There are three (3) electrical systems on a recreational vehicle; AC (alternating current, like in the house), DC (direct current, like a battery) for the Coach and Chassis. In some recreational vehicles the DC circuits will overlap and share components like the battery. But they still exists. I am not going to cover basic electrical theory here. In fact, you will not be doing much testing of these circuits at all. For the most part you will be checking to see if the lights, appliances, fans and other electronics work properly. You will perform a visual check of the electrical components including the power cords, protection circuits such as fuses, circuit breakers and GFCI protection.

To begin the inspection of the electrical system, start with the outside power connections. Verify that the power cord is in good shape. There should be no burn marks, repairs or modification to the cord. Follow it to the connection on the rig.

From here almost every rig will be different. Some will have a surge protection device some won't. Some will have an inverter or converter or both, others will not have either. Inverters convert the battery power to AC current to run things like TV and air conditioners when the power goes out. Converters charge the batteries from the electric coming into the rig from the power pole. Surge Protectors protect all the electronics from power related issues like lightning strikes, brownouts and accidents. If the recreational vehicle does not have surge protection it is a great idea to get one. I won't make any recommendations here. Search Facebook for what people have found useful.

Let's start with the biggest testing area inside the recreational vehicle, the GFCI Circuit Test. For this you will need that 3 prong AC Circuit tester. This is the thing with 3 lights on it that plugs into the wall outlets. Starting at the electrical pole, plug in the tester into the 120 volt plug if there is one. It should test good. If not, there is a wiring problem at the pole and do not attempt to power up the recreational vehicle until it is corrected. If it passes, go into the recreational vehicle and from the front, find and test every outlet. If there are two plugs together, test them both. Record on your inspection sheet any outlet that does not pass.

Now, find the GFCI breaker. It will be in one of three places, either the kitchen sink area, the bathroom, or in the circuit breaker box. Normally it will be an electrical outlet with two push buttons in the center. One will say test. Press it. Once it trips, go back and test every outlet again. Some will no longer work. Note those that don't work on the back of the report. This is great information to have. You will save a lot of time knowing which outlets are covered by this circuit when it is dark out and something trips the GFCI circuit.

With the GFCI testing done, turn on and off every light, fan, and electrical appliance. Make sure they all work. Record anything that does not work as it should.

Check the circuit breaker box. Are all circuit breakers set properly? Some units will also have an automotive fuse box located with the circuit breakers. Check those as well. It will be a great idea to find and identify all the fuses in your rig. Read my story of the $2,500.00 fuse on my blog site at http://our-rv-adventures.com. Hopefully, you won't have the same issue.

There is a chance that there will be a problem with the rig you won't be testing for. It is call a Hot Skin Test. A hot skin is caused by a tapping into either a 12 v DC hot wire or a 120 v AC hot wire. This in effect causes the frame of the recreational vehicle to be grounded, so when you touch any metal on the recreational vehicle you complete the electrical circuit causing something from a tingle to an actual shock when you enter the recreational vehicle. If you notice any sensation upon entering the vehicle that doesn't appear normal, I would recommend that you turn off the power at the pole and contact an electrician or rv mechanic immediately to test for Hot Skin. The reason we are not going to do it here is that it takes equipment you might not have and a special testing setup.

Once you have tested all equipment, lights (both inside and outside, don't forget the storage area lights), fans and GFCI circuits, it is time to move on to the generator (if the rig has one).

Generator

Before starting the generator the vehicle must have at least 1/4 tank of fuel. The manufacturer does this to make sure you don't run out of fuel when camping and can't get to the gas station to fill up. The last thing you want is to run the tank dry in the middle of the night and have to call the towing service to bring you some fuel.

There will probably be several places where you can start the generator. For the first test, we will start outside at the generator itself. Start by checking the oil and coolant. This is a good idea anytime the rig has been setting for any period of time. Also, now is a good time to record the hours of operation, if there is a meter for that. I would also recommend that you perform a fluid analysis on the generator as well. Yes I know it another $60 or so, but the generator can be a very handy piece of equipment to have around and you want to make sure you are getting your money's worth.

Once all the checks and recording of information is completed, the next step is to determine if you have to hook up anything to it. Some units require that you plug in the rig to the generator. Ask the seller for help if you're not sure. Other systems have an automatic switch that will transfer the generator power to the rig once it has stabilized. Now it is time to start the generator. Press and hold the start button. If the coach batteries are in good shape the generator should start. Once it is turned on, make sure the circuit breakers on the generator are on and go inside the rig.

Time to put some load on the generator. Turn on the air conditioner or any heavy electrical load (electric heaters etc.). Run the generator for a few minutes to make sure it has no issues and then power down the electric items you turned on and turn off the generator.

If the rig has an Inverter that will be the next test.

Inverter

Before starting the inverter testing let's check on the batteries. Again, the idea of the inverter is to convert the battery voltage and current to AC voltage/current that can be used to power the TV, air conditioners, microwave and other AC components. Not all rigs will have an inverter. Those that do will have a separate set of house batteries normally. These may be 12 volt or 6 volt batteries. Find out where they are stored and examine them. Look for water levels, corrosion, loose cables etc. See if they are all the same rating (size), same age, etc. You do not want to mix old and new batteries. The old batteries will destroy the new and you will end up replacing all of them. There may be a battery cutoff switch. If so, make sure it is on.

NOTE: If you know how to read a multi-meter and have one available, you can check the voltage at each battery.

Converter

With the battery check done, let's turn on the inverter. The control could be anywhere. Ask the owner for help. You are looking for the ability of the inverter to carry the load. Turn on the TV or air conditioner and microwave to make sure they work. The age, size and charge level of the batteries and the draw (number of items turned on) will determine how long the items will operate. For this test we just want to make sure it works.

When you turn off the inverter the next thing that should happen is the converter should kick on. The purpose of the converter is to take the AC from the pole or generator and charge the house/coach batteries. So make sure you restore power from the pole after testing the inverter. Remember, the last test we did for power was to start the generator. You may have to remove the power cord and normalize the AC cables.

With power restored the Converter should show that it is charging the batteries. If not, make a note and let a qualified technician look at it.

Water Systems

To test the water systems you will need access to city water and a food grade water hose. Food grade water hoses are normally white on the outside. I highly recommend that you also have a pressure regulator. These will limit the amount of water pressure to the rig so that your internal water lines don't blow out due to high water pressure. We have been places that the water pressure has been over 100 psi. Normal water pressure is usually less than 60 psi. The water regulators limit the pressure to around 40-50 psi.

With the water connected start by checking the cold water pressure and flow at an outside faucet if one is available. Then move inside and check the bathroom sink, toilet, shower and kitchen. We only want to check cold at this point. We still have to check out the hot water system which is coming up next.

Water Heater

Water heaters are beginning to get complicated. It used to be, and the majority still are, built by two companies, Atwood and Suburban. Atwood used aluminum tanks and Suburban steel. Because of the steel tank, Suburban heaters have an Anode rod that should be replaced at least every other year or when it wears out. Lately two other water heaters have come on the market. One is the tankless water heater or on demand and the other is the Aqua Hot System. Aqua hot is a combination heater/water heater and will only be found in high end units at this time. Regardless of the water heater type the testing is the same. Make sure water, propane and electric are available. Ensure the water tank is filled with water and turn on the unit. Wait about 30 minutes for the tank to heat up. Turn on the hot water.

With the thermometer, check and record the temperature. It should be about 140 degrees. Some older units may not have an automatic pilot and you will have to manually light them. Make sure you have a butane lighter like the ones use to like charcoal fires with you just in case.

Check the water heater for bugs and debris. Also check that it has water in it (many units have a bypass valve behind the water heater, make sure it is not in bypass). It is very important to have water in the heater before turning it on. Failure to do so will burn out the water heater. Some units have a valve on the water heater that you can open. Be careful. If the heater has been on the water inside will be under pressure and hot!

Record the information on the water heater and head inside. If you turned on the water heater it may take a few minutes before the water gets hot. Come back and test it after about 15 minutes or so. Once inside, start with the bathroom sink and check for hot water flow and temperature. If you don't have a digital thermometer just make sure it gets warm. You may want to add cold water first and then turn off the cold until the water is warm. Please use caution, the water temperature may exceed 140 degrees F.

Waste Water System

To test the waste water systems you will need to be hooked up to either the sewer system or a portable sewer system (commonly called a blue tank). Starting on the outside of the rig, make sure that the cap is over the dump valve and that the sewer hose is not connected. You want to close both valves on the rig and run some water into the systems. Cold water is fine. Run a couple of gallons into both the toilet and the sink. Now remove the cap, DO NOT OPEN THE VALVES. This test to make sure that the valves are working and not leaking. If water should pour out of the system one or both of the valves are bad.

Hook up the sewer hose and dump the black tank first. Once the water has drained out, close the valve and open the gray tank valve. When that water is drained close the gray tank valve. There may be more than one gray tank. Repeat the test for the other tanks as well. Sometimes with fifth wheels the washing machine or other bathrooms may have their own systems.

Propane /LP/ CO / Smoke Detectors

The propane system consists of the tanks, lines, propane detector, stove, oven, water heater and furnace. There are two types of propane tanks. DOT regulated and ASME. On motor homes or Class type RVs (Drivable), the ASME tanks are the primary means of storing propane. These tanks do not need to be replaced and are 'inspected' by the person that fills them with propane. Normally these will be rated in gallons of propane and not pounds. For your inspection, you want to make sure that the tank appears to be in good condition. Also check the piping coming out of the tank for loose connections. Your nose is the best test equipment. Make sure the tank is on and smell for propane (rotten eggs).

The DOT tanks come in 20 lbs., 30 lbs. and 40 lbs. for RV. There are larger sizes but you won't find them in the RV. You may have 1 or 2 tanks. I haven't seen more than 2 in any RV yet, but that doesn't mean they can't have them. DOT tanks are rated for 12 years of life and will have a manufactures date stamped on the top crown of the tank. It then must be inspected and re-certified. It will then be good for another 5 years. After 17 years they must be replaced.

If the system has two tanks, the regulator will probably be an automatic switch over type. You will be able to recognize this type of regulator as it will have a red/green indicator showing that you have propane in the online tank and a switch to change from one tank to the other. When the online tank (the one the switch is set to) is empty, the indicator will be red. You can then switch the tank selector to the other tank and remove the empty bottle for filling.

As a professional RV inspector, we do a pressure test on the propane system. If you detect a leak, turn off the propane and call a qualified technician to check it out. If the tanks (DOT) are out of date or close to expiration dates, you will want these replaced.

LP Detector

Every rig is required to have an LP detector. They are normally located near the floor or below waist level. These are good for 7 years. There is usually a manufacture date stamped on the back. Some newer units will have the date on the front. Make sure the detector is current.

You can perform a simple LP detector test with a butane lighter. Simply click the lighter but do not light the flame. Put the lighter down near the LP detector. It should go off within a minute or so. If it does not, there is a likelihood that it is bad, especially if it is out of date. Butane, propane and methane are all related gases and will set off the LP detector. NOTE: so will the dog/cat if they have gas.

Smoke Detector

Unless you are a smoker, there isn't much to test. There should be a date of manufacture on the back of the unit along with make and model. Record this information. If you are a smoker you can blow smoke into the detector to see if it goes off. Not a great test but a start.

CO Detector

Unless the rig has an engine you may not have a CO detector. Most travel trailers and fifth wheels, for example, will not. However, if you have a toy hauler or Class vehicle you will. The purpose of the CO detect is to detect fumes from the engine compartment. There is no easy test for these so just record the information. As with the other detectors 7 years is the limit. CO Detectors are expensive running around $95.00.

Appliances

Refrigerator

There used to be two types of refrigerators: absorption with helium and absorption with hydrogen. Today a lot of manufacturers are switching over to residential style refrigerators. Regardless of the type, your inspection and testing will be the same. Does it cool? The checklist at the end of this book does ask you the type and for the most part it will be either residential or Hydrogen Absorption. The big difference for you is the recreational vehicle style refrigerators will operate off of propane or electric while the residential will only operate off of AC.

To test the refrigerators you are mainly looking at will it cool. This test needs some time. Hopefully, the refrigerator was turned on prior to starting the testing. If so a few hours have passed and you should be able to determine if the refrigerator is beginning to cool. Place your hand in the upper left hand corner of the freezer. Is it cool/cold? If so, do the same thing to the lower compartment. Is it cool/cold? If the answer is yes, then the refrigerator is working.

Furnace

Depending on the time of year this one could be as difficult as the air conditioners. The furnace in an RV is a pretty simple device. It contains a burning chamber, a fan, a controller and an igniter. The system starts by turning on the blower. There is a sail switch that detects if it is blowing air. Once the air is detected the controller board opens the valve for the propane and tries to ignite it. There is a temperature sensor that detects the heat. If after 10 seconds no heat is detected, the system shuts down in most cases. So for inspecting, first open the outside door and check for bugs. They love the propane smell it seems. Then make sure the propane is on and turn on the heater. Listen and feel for the fan operation. You should then hear the whoosh of the propane igniting. Finally the heat should come out of the vents. Pretty simple test.

Cook Top

Do I really need to describe how to test a stove? Well I guess there are some people who don't work with propane stoves very often. Anyway, make sure the propane is on. Turn one of the knobs to light and hit the igniter. Some old stoves may not have an igniter and some may have an igniter that is bad. So in that case use a lighter or match. There really isn't much that can go wrong with a propane stove. Replacement is the repair process.

Air Conditioner

Here is the test I would be doing if you had me inspecting the air conditioner.

When looking at an RV you will want to run the Air Conditioners for at least 10 minutes. Then with a food grade thermometer take the temperature of the incoming air (about 5 minutes) and then at the vent closest to the air conditioner take the outgoing air temperature. You are looking for a difference in temperature of about 20 degrees F or more.

If you have the digital thermometer you can do the same test. Otherwise, place your hand near one of the vents when the AC has been on for at least 10 minutes. Is the air cooler than what is in the room? Document your results. NOTE: the AC units in these rigs are not repairable. If it goes bad, you replace the whole unit.

Interior

Ceiling, Walls and Floor

This set of inspections will probably take the longest for the inside of the rig. Really careful attention needs to be paid to those areas where you identified possible problems on the roof. As I stated before, water from the roof will run down the walls. So while doing this inspection you will be looking closely at the roof, walls and floors of the rig to determine if there is any damage that might indicate rot or water damage. In all honesty, this is another 'Deal Breaker' if it is found, so pay very close attention to the details.

Starting at the same corner that you started on the roof and exterior, examine the ceiling for water marks, discoloration, softness and repairs. Is the trim missing or damaged? Work your way down the walls from top to bottom. Check around windows and doorways for water damage, discoloration, repairs etc. Note and take pictures of anything that looks strange or out of place. Continue to the floors. Is the carpet discolored, brittle, torn? Is the floor under the carpet solid or are there weak spots?

Cabinets

Open each cabinet door and all the drawers. Inspect the hinges and slides. Are there any problems? Do the doors and drawers close and lock in place? That is right they should lock in place. Unlike a house, the drawers and doors lock in place to prevent items inside from flying out when you stop suddenly or turn a sharp corner. Look at the walls behind the cabinets for signs of damage or repairs.

Blinds and Shades

You will want to test every shade/blind. These are different than a house blind or shade in most cases. Recreational vehicles come with day/night shades and most RV owners have a love/hate relationship with them. Make sure they go up and stay up. They are a two part shade, the top part is for dark and the bottom for light. Look for damage, water marks, or broken strings on shades that don't work.

Furniture

Now comes the comfortable part, checking the furniture. Depending on the purpose of the RV you may be removing what is currently installed and therefore don't care about the condition. However, if you plan on keeping this rig and it furniture then by all means check it out. I like to give it a good look over and then sit in the chairs and on the sofa. Pretend you are going to watch TV. On the sofa sit on the ends and in the middle. If it is a sleeper sofa, open it up and check the condition of the mattress.

Some kitchen tables are collapsible. Do it! Make sure everything works the way it is suppose to. Note anything that needs attention.

So, now you have inspected what I hope is the perfect recreational vehicle for you. You can sit down with the seller and go over any major items determine who will be responsible for the repairs and if need be negotiate a better price.

Checklist

I did not include the checklist in this book because of the format and the fact that you may be looking at more than one recreational vehicle and need multiple copies. The checklist available on the website are much more detailed than what could be printed in this book.

Checklist for Buying the Perfect RV are available free of charge on our website at http://rv-inspection-service.com/book-store.

Made in the USA
Middletown, DE
09 August 2015